THINK V

G000075228

THINK WITH ME

Fundamentals for making our country ideal

'Saharasri' Subrata Roy Sahara

RUPA

Published by
Rupa Publications India Pvt. Ltd 2016
7/16, Ansari Road, Daryaganj
New Delhi 110002

Sales Centres:
Allahabad Bengaluru Chennai
Hyderabad Jaipur Kathmandu
Kolkata Mumbai

ISBN: 978-81-291-4225-2

First impression 2016

10 9 8 7 6 5 4 3 2 1

The moral right of the author has been asserted.

Printed by Replika Press Pvt. Ltd, India

**Dedicated To My Most
Revered Mother
Late Smt. Chhabi Roy**

O Deeply Revered Mother!
You were truly beyond compare
You brought us up with such love, such affection
and instilled in us such high morals and values
that they strengthened our inner core, gave us our
self-respect
they illumined the path of our collective growth

O Benevolent Mother,
You overflowed with compassion
but were strongly adherent to principles
We learnt from you the first lessons in discipline
and to be motivated towards our definite goals
O pious Mother, we always found in You the
greatest Teacher
You enlightened us to adorn our thoughts with a
positive attitude
to always look for goodness in others and
to absorb the goodness of all others in our actions
Your lesson to us was to care for others
and to comfort all those in pain who suffer

O Loving Mother,
You were an able philosopher
From You we learnt about the unique joy
that one experiences in giving something to others
that one must give from the heart as it is in our
hands
but never be anxious to receive as it lies in the
hands of others
You taught us to always perform our duties
religiously
without getting worried or being gripped by
confusion
to remain free of stress even in the face of adversity

O Divine Mother,
You will live in our hearts forever
Your blessings will always give us soothing comfort
And whenever we look back in cherished
remembrance
Your blissful image will fill us with immense
happiness

Ever yours
Chandan
('Saharasri' Subrata Roy Sahara)

CONTENTS

PREFACE

You all are well aware that I am a corporate person. A question may stir your mind as to why a corporate man who is supposed to write about industry, trade, marketing and other financial issues, is voicing his views on politics, religion, education etc. I would like to state the reasons by connecting my answer to our glorious struggle for Independence.

Our long war of freedom was not simply aimed at grabbing power from the clutches of foreigners or chasing them away from our land. The great leadership that had emerged during the struggle had a pious dream for Independent India. This dream was the dream of the whole country—of all of us. Our dream was that India would rise as an advanced, progressive and prosperous country wherein people would live together in harmony, work collectively, achieve collectively and the collective gains would be distributed equitably, filling people's lives with abundant peace, happiness and satisfaction.

Though India had to go through the most traumatic moment of its history when it got partitioned on communal lines, Independent India, nevertheless, chose to run its polity democratically, where all the citizens got equal rights constitutionally, including the most important right i.e. the right to vote. We wanted our diverse Indian society, which had been nurturing many religions, castes and sub-castes, regions and languages, to exist in peace, shedding all deep-rooted prejudices, discord, enmities and hatred.

There is no doubt that India has made rapid progress and achieved prosperity too, yet the goals that we set for ourselves are still unfulfilled or underachieved. It is a harsh reality that we have bigger problems today than we had at the time of Independence. These problems are not good signs for the future of India.

During the freedom struggle, a class of honest, hard working and dedicated leaders rose all across the country, leaders who presented their lives as exemplary for others. What kind of leadership is emerging these days? Where has this leadership taken us? Though people vote for this or that bunch of leaders, yet they have little faith in them and always doubt their integrity.

Rapid and uncontrolled growth of population is one of the biggest issues of our country. At the time of Independence, our population was around 36 crore which has now crossed the 130 crore mark. The actual problem lies in the inferior kind of growth. Don't you think that some very effective measures are needed to check this unhealthy trend?

We never wanted to produce only clerks through our education system, instead we wanted it to develop our people wholesomely, allow their personality to grow and prosper on human virtues and make them responsible citizens of a civilized country. Is our education system anywhere close to achieving this objective?

When we adopted a democratic system with the judiciary, the legislature and the executive as its three pillars, we naturally imagined the media as the fourth pillar which would keep a constant vigil on the functioning of the other three, give people correct and relevant information, make them aware of things happening around them and instill a sense of positivism in their minds. Thus, the media was to serve as the guide and teacher of the people. Is the present media serving this purpose?

We may claim to be a secular society but the truth is that the whole Indian society is ravaged by communal tensions. Communal riots and religion-instigated terrorism have become common occurrences these days. Religion related distortions are continuously on the rise, so much so that the internal security of the country is in grave danger. Have we found an appropriate solution to this problem yet?

When we see the problems related to political leadership, population growth, education, the media and religion going from bad to worse, a natural question comes up in our minds. Where, after all, did we go wrong? What happened during our democratic journey of independent India that we are faced with nasty problems on all these fronts? Why couldn't we teach people occupying places of responsibility that rights are given to perform your genuine duties, not to serve your personal whims, false ego and greed? Owing to the irresponsible attitude of responsible people, honest and law-abiding citizens are increasingly facing up to immense difficulties. We all know, if these problems continue to be as they are, they will create a severe crisis for the country and its people in the near future. Should not we then think over these problems honestly and sincerely?

Yes, I do agree that I am a corporate person and am proud of the fact that I am the Guardian of the great Sahara India Pariwar which has more than 12 lac dedicated workers in its family fold. But, even before that, I am a true and conscientious citizen of my beloved country, who loves his 'Bharat Maa' from the core of his heart. In this capacity I have always been thinking about the severe problems our country is faced with.

Whatever problems I have mentioned here, I have formed certain ideas about them, which I have presented in this book. I am no authority on these subjects, nor have I ever claimed to be so, yet, to observe and learn from everyone and make others learn too has always been a part of my nature. In this way, whatever ideas I have developed, I am honestly presenting before you. It doesn't matter whether you agree with me or not, however, it is certain that the thoughts and ideas expressed in the book would compel you to think deep, to ponder over, and then you too would come to the conclusion that if nothing concrete is done at the earliest we would be in the grip of difficulties and problems of mammoth proportions.

Whatever I have thought and concluded about the above mentioned subjects I want to share with you all, particularly with those who are occupying the higher posts of leadership and decision-making. If this book of mine is helpful in producing even the slightest of positive thinking among its readers and inspires or provokes them into thinking in the interest of our country, I will feel proud and take my effort as successful.

Emotionally yours
'Saharasri' Subrata Roy Sahara

Electoral System & Leadership

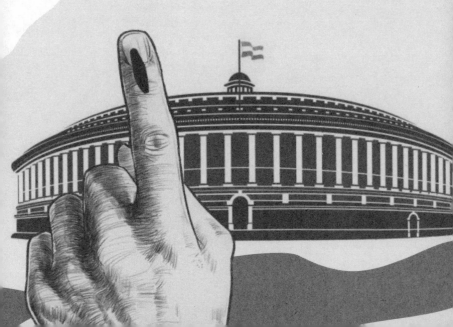

For any democratic set-up to function properly the need is for strong public leaders as it is they who form a Government on the basis of majority and are the ones who formulate laws and rules for the benefit of the nation, just as the people's participation in the system of governance carries equal importance. It is therefore, expected that these public leaders are able, honest and ethical, whose emotional sphere is so wide as to accommodate people from all strata within its folds.

1. Electoral System & Leadership

We are the proud citizens of the world's largest democracy. For any democratic set-up to function properly the need is for strong public leaders as it is they who form a government on the basis of majority and are the ones who formulate laws and rules for the benefit of the nation, just as the people's participation in the system of governance carries equal importance. It is therefore, expected that these public leaders are able, honest and ethical, whose emotional sphere is so wide as to accommodate people from all strata within its folds.

But today the situation seems to be turning to just the opposite. People with confined spheres are in the place of leadership. Such of those leaders as were found before Independence, who strove for a strong democracy and democratic culture are generally not to be seen anymore. Leaders of that period followed ethical values and lived by those values only. But today, unethical people with confined emotional spheres have come to occupy positions of leadership.

A true democratic system calls for holding free and fair elections whenever the legitimate tenure of a constituency draws to a close. But is that followed in spirit and norm? Is our election system flawed or laden with impenetrable complexity? Is wasteful expenditure to win elections at all costs eroding our democratic values and striking at the very roots of our constitutional framework?

Today, it is important to understand why all this is happening. In this chapter, I have taken up the twin issues of the electoral system and leadership as the two are basically inter-related.

PERSONS OF A CONFINED SPHERE ARE HARMFUL IN POSITIONS OF LEADERSHIP

Immorality and Morality: People with High Moral Values and Immoral Values

You are well aware that if a man holding a small responsibility does not fulfill his duties well, he causes a loss howsoever small it may be, but if a man holding a big responsibility does not perform his duties satisfactorily he is likely to cause a bigger loss. Therefore, if the individual sphere of those holding a significant responsibility of providing leadership or being guardians does not expand permanently in proportion to the sphere of their responsibility, it creates a distressing and dangerous situation.

Let me explain by first telling you that I divide the emotional sphere of a human being into five categories, namely 'I', 'My', 'We', 'We All' and 'Us'.

'I' represents a confined emotional sphere restricted to oneself; 'My' represents a limited emotional sphere which extends to the immediate members of the family that include the mother, the father, the husband, the wife, the children, etc.; 'We' represents a large and satisfactory emotional sphere that includes one's work place from where one earns his livelihood and other material things along with respect; 'We All' extends to the country and the society to which a person belongs, meaning where one derives emotional satisfaction in the performance of genuine duties so as to fulfil the needs and desires of a country (i.e. the countrymen); and 'Us' represents a vast and expansive emotional sphere that envelopes the entire humanity.

People who hold high positions of responsibility i.e. covering a wider ambit of the society, region or nation as leaders or guardians, if live in a very narrow sphere of 'I', wreak havoc and destruction across all the three spheres. These persons of a limited sphere of 'I' and 'My' lead the society, state or even the nation into a state of chaos and disorder. If these leaders remain confined to the sphere of 'I' and 'My', they cannot do justice to the society, state or nation.

Until and unless the emotional sphere of the people occupying positions of leadership expands to the extent that the people of the society, the region or the nation come within its ambit on a permanent basis, they will neither have the desire nor will they be able to deliver justice, through their actions-reactions, their planning, decisions and directions.

You can grasp this matter well in another way too. These days often people ask where the dedicated people such as the ones who got our country liberated have disappeared. I do understand the fact that in every place in the world and in every era there have been people of a large emotional sphere i.e. of high moral values and they will always be there in future too; and along with them will exist people of immoral values, i.e. the people living in a narrow and limited sphere of 'I' or 'My'.

The people with high moral values are those whose emotional sphere remains emotionally connected and on a permanent basis, with the multitudes, and because they are emotionally attached, they get emotional satisfaction in fulfilling their duty towards them judiciously, by doing good for them, relentlessly, day and night. Moral people always desire to achieve this kind of satisfaction, and if they are unable to do good to the people they are dissatisfied, something which they want to keep away from as that leads to emotional dissatisfaction, which becomes poison for the internal personality [i.e. spiritual personality].

In such situations where the multitudes rightfully benefit from a person with a large emotional sphere, they call him a man of 'moral values'. And contrary to this when the multitude is continuously harmed by the people living in a very narrow sphere of 'I' and hankering for the dominance of their 'I' i.e. of their post and designation, and regularly suffers from their actions and reactions, their planning and decisions, etc., it terms such people as those with 'immoral values'. There are different categories of moral as well as immoral people.

Here I would like to cite the example of a father who was like God to his two children but quite a monster at his workplace, where he was considered a man with immoral values. The son and the daughter were placed permanently within the father's confined emotional sphere. This father left no stone unturned in raising his son and daughter in order to get the food of emotional satisfaction. The son and the daughter too, dedicatedly and enthusiastically (being fully and permanently involved emotionally) kept fulfilling their duties. The father too fulfilled his duties enthusiastically and dedicatedly (being fully emotionally involved) towards his son and daughter. The son and the daughter had a very good life. The son was well settled and the daughter was grandly married off. She settled down to a good life too.

When the son and daughter were asked who the most moralistic person in the world was or was equivalent to God for them, they both in the same breath named their father and rated him on a par with God.

But when the people at his workplace were asked, they all said in unison that he was a man with immoral values, one who never devotedly worked for the organization and placed the interest of his family before the interest of the organization, goofed up at the work place and involved himself only in the welfare of his family, meaning thereby, he was involved only in thinking and doing good to his family members (his son and daughter). In the emotional sphere of this father only the kith and kin (the son and daughter, etc.) were placed and he could never expand his 'I' and his 'My' any further to include the organization.

It may now be clearly understood that a man fulfils his duties dedicatedly and according to the demand of time only towards the people within his emotional sphere without any expectations and with full devotion. And the people inside the emotional sphere benefit continuously without having any expectations in return. So the beneficiaries upon getting excessive benefits see their father as God incarnate but since the organization does not gain any advantage because of that father's narrow sphere, or rather suffers loss, the people in the organisation consider this man as good-for-nothing, immoral and devil incarnate.

When someone confers benefits on the people with the purpose of fulfilling his duty towards them without any expectation, he is called a benefactor and a moralistic person.

Now, it can be clearly understood that responsible people sitting at responsible posts to perform their duties in the field of Legislature, Judiciary, Bureaucracy, Education, the Corporate World and the Media, having a confined and limited emotional sphere are dangerous for the society and the nation. Here I shall strongly comment and recommend that besides all exams and selection systems, A PROPER MEASURE OR APPRAISAL OF THIS EMOTIONAL SPHERE SHOULD BE IN ORDER AND NEEDS TO BE STRICTLY CARRIED OUT (I can personally guide the method) along with regular education of life which should be imparted among all such people.

Gandhiji was called the 'Father of The Nation' because his emotional sphere was so large that the whole nation came into it permanently, and therefore his duties were focused on the welfare of the whole country and its people. In the same way Gautam Buddha's emotional sphere expanded to an extent that it encompassed the entire humanity permanently, and he was called God.

Therefore, in order to lead a beautiful and grand life with peace, happiness and satisfaction or to get the desired money, respect and love to lead to a full sense of security (*I have explained this aspect in detail in my earlier book, 'Life Mantras'*), it must be noted that there may be a person who does not desire money more than respect, and there may be another person who does not care for respect as much as he cares for money. But in the people with a large emotional sphere it is often seen that their desire for money is only in accordance with their need i.e. it is very less comparatively. Rather they need food of emotional satisfaction in abundance because the internal personality [i.e. spiritual personality] of such people is always larger than their external personality, and therefore their priority lies in getting the satisfaction of love, i.e. they want to get emotional satisfaction continuously. This is in the continuous and enthusiastic performance of all genuine duties towards others.

On the other hand, emotionally confined people do not know their duties; they know their rights very well but are ignorant of the fact that rights are given to perform genuine duties and not to serve personal whims, fancies or greed. This can be likened to a soldier posted at the border who kills hundreds of enemies and get a gallantry award, however, if the same soldier kills a person in his village over a land dispute, he is condemned to death by hanging. He has been given a weapon to be used as a means to carry out his genuine duties at the border, not to help serve his personal whims.

LEADERSHIP BEFORE AND AFTER INDEPENDENCE: ELECTION EXPENSES

If you have ever discussed about the nation and the society you must have talked about Independence. You might have drawn comparisons between the pre- and post-Independence conditions, between the personalities of the leaders—then and now. You might have realized that people in those early years were fairly moral.

Nevertheless, I would like to say that even before Independence, from the point of view of the nation, along with the people of high moral values i.e. of a large emotional sphere, a majority of people were those having immoral values, i.e. having a confined or a limited emotional sphere. Because moral people were less in number (I have so observed that at every place in the world the people of moral values are always in minority) and the number of people with immoral values was far larger, it took so long to achieve Independence.

As the immoral people love only the sphere of their 'I' or 'My' or at the most their 'We', they have no lasting love for the society, region or their motherland. In most matters they are very opportunistic. It does not matter to them whether the country is enslaved or independent. Only the business of their own bread and butter, the pleasures or the good things of life, matter to them.

In whatever sphere a man lives emotionally, he gives priority to fulfilling his duty towards only those people who fall within his emotional sphere. He gives importance to people outside his sphere only when they serve his own purpose or he wants to avoid some impending losses. He is very calculative in such matters.

Before Independence the people with morality that is, a large emotional sphere, who were at the forefront knew very well that at any moment a bullet might hit them, or their families might be ruined during the freedom movement. Despite all these impending dangers, their emotions had such a large sphere and they were of such a high moral category that the

British bullets failed to check their surging energies. This was the acid test before Independence for separating the moral from the immoral. The people with high moral values [like the great 'Netas'] had an emotional sphere large enough to make them move forward and they provided leadership without thinking about the British bullets. In this way the people of moral values with large emotional spheres filtered through the struggle for Independence. They were very few in number though.

But when the sun of Independence dawned, the fear of bullets also disappeared. In the beginning of the mission of building the nation, the people of high moral values carried out electioneering on cycles and bullock carts and got elected at very nominal election expenditure. As the years rolled by, the election expenses went on increasing. Today in a single constituency crores of rupees are squandered away. So much so that many of the morally inclined people, with their self-esteem at stake, refuse to raise the lacs and crores of rupees that are required to contest elections today, either by begging or other foul means. In the present situation there are two categories of moral people who are able to fight elections—the ones who have inherited millions or billions of rupees from their forefathers, have won a lottery worth that much amount or have been associated with politics over 20, 30, 40, even 50 years.

Children are reared in the emotional sphere of a mother and father. Due to the emotional bonding, the parents always do justice to their children. They can never do any kind of injustice which may harm them. They cannot go out on a holiday or a picnic by sidestepping the school fees of their children. They cannot wish for a crown at the cost of their children's ruin. They cannot lust for fashionable clothes by keeping their children naked. At the same time the parents would never like to feel humiliated, insulted or to let their self esteem be lowered in the eyes of their children (with whom their emotional involvement is permanent). In order to fulfill their desires for clothes and other possessions they will never resort to begging, stealing, cheating etc. By saying this I want to emphasize upon the fact that a man is always self-respecting within a sphere where his emotions are involved.

Likewise, the people whose emotional sphere encompasses the society, region and nation are moral people who always maintain self-respect and self-esteem with regard to the very society, region and the nation they are connected with (or else the feeling of dissatisfaction; of lack of respect troubles them, saps their strength). Every human being wishes to keep himself away from emotional dissatisfaction, and for that he does whatever he has to.

MORAL AND IMMORAL PEOPLE MAKE DIFFERENT USE OF THE ELECTORAL SYSTEM

So the moral people keep themselves away from elections or

suppress their desire to serve the country by winning an election because, unlike immoral people, they can neither beg for crores of rupees nor can they become race-horses. Meaning thereof, they refuse to win an election today by taking monetary favors from anybody, lest they are tempted to serve the interests of those who gave them money, after coming to power thus, betraying the minor and major duties towards the nation and the society. People with a large emotional sphere, that is, the moral people never do so.

As I said, before Independence the people of moral values filtered through a hard struggle, through examinations. Today election expenditure has increased to crores of rupees, besides which, violence has become an inevitable part of electioneering.

Following Independence, people of immoral values, the ones belonging to the opportunist class, which, during the British period, ate, drank and made merry, have begun to come up through unscrupulous means and methods and started grabbing leadership positions. It means, people with an opportunistic behavior, the kind who were left behind in obscurity before Independence, have now, by the power of gun and by the power of money, risen to prominence by occupying the leadership slot.

So before Independence, the examination for leadership was for those emotionally large-sphered people who were ready to take bullets on the chest; just like a mother who is willing to do so for the sake of her child. But the examination for leadership today is for those who can generate money in the most wrongful manner, those who thrive by the bullet and organize criminal elements, etc.

My concern for any nation or its people is not that people with a large and expansive emotional sphere or with moral values, are not occupying positions of leadership as many such people are there even today but for the fact that proportionately, those with a small or restricted emotional sphere with immoral values are continuously filtering in, in large numbers.

FEELING OF INSECURITY IN PEOPLE PROVIDING LEADERSHIP OWING TO THE FREQUENCY OF ELECTIONS BEING HELD

First let me explain to you a marked tendency, that I have observed among people, to exhibit their status and authority which I feel is a direct offshoot of a feeling of insecurity that grips them. In other words, when occupying plum posts, they make a pomp and show of their authority owing to their being inherently insecure as individuals. The insecurity stems from a fear of losing out on their posts, and consequently, their power and influence one day and thereafter, having nothing to show to the others.

I recall the instance of a former Aviation Minister who took immense pride in himself and always liked to impress upon others his rank and stature as an individual. Once he arrived at an airport with a cavalcade of vehicles as he loved showing off the power and authority at his command, which saw people in great numbers attending to his protocol. A huge gathering was there to welcome him and he felt visibly pleased at all the attention. Later when he ceased to be the Aviation Minister, I again saw him arrive at the airport but this time, all by himself in a modest Fiat car without his accompanying staff. This was because having been divested of his responsibility as a Minister, thereby losing his status and authority, he had nothing to show to the others. So he kept his arrival a low-key affair as the fear of being recognised in public only as a former Aviation Minister and not as a person of rank or authority, made him feel highly insecure as an individual.

Today, a similar feeling of insecurity is very much prevalent in people providing leadership, because elections are held only after five years or there are apprehensions of elections being held mid-term, hence such people out of selfishness, desire to achieve the maximum from just one election term. Therefore, their indifference towards their duties is on an alarming rise.

Here, we can ask who is responsible for all this. I will only say that for such conditions as prevalent today, the ones who should be held responsible are the people who are providing leadership themselves. When they will be weak and incorrect in fulfilling their short term and long term duties in the interest of the masses, the masses will try to defeat one and make the other victorious, or defeat the second but try to make the first or the third victorious, or would try to defeat the third and try and reach out to the fourth or the fifth, in the vain hope that there will at least be someone who will satisfy their 'I'. After listening to brilliant and captivating lectures of leaders of new parties and their tirade against the existing government in power, voters begin to see the reflection of their bright future in the new parties and leaders.

Here I state vehemently that unless and until there is a manifestation of ethical values among leaders, there should be a legal prohibition for all political leaders on using the mike for delivering lectures or deriving any kind of publicity based on their lectures. Whatever they have to say they should distribute it in that particular region through black and white handbills, bearing the signature of the writers (should be attested by two competent authorities) and the signatures of the witnesses. The local newspaper should lawfully document them through regional publications, as per the requirement.

INCREASED EXPENDITURE DURING ELECTIONS– A DISTURBING TREND

No doubt, on the whole, a democratic system is the best for a beautiful co-existence of the human society. But in view of the excessive spending on elections, all those unethical leaders with confined spheres are using the democratic system as a bad instrument, akin to a gun. Who knows when and where it will be fired! It is being continuously fired and the foundation of the personality of our beloved country, with wonderful values, beliefs and tradition, is being weakened on account of being targeted over and over again.

As the election expenses are visibly mounting, it is inevitable that people with confined spheres, who are thieves, ruffians would reach the positions of leadership by winning elections using their financial clout and that is exactly what is happening. I need to mention that if the election expenses continue to rise then people with ethical values are bound to be displaced, thrown out of the positions of leadership while people with unethical values will openly acquire those very political chairs.

Here, it is also important to understand that people small or big, who are in a confined sphere of their 'I' and who accumulate wealth through unfair and wrongful means, are always a point of interest for anti-social elements, scoundrels who tend to stick to them like ants. Gradually, unethical people who are in the positions of leadership too give sufficient importance to such anti-social elements in their quest to satisfy their confined 'I'. This is the influence of such anti-social elements which is prevalent to quite an extent and is creating a perilous situation all-round.

Another thing that needs to be understood is that this sequence will go on unchecked because elections have to be held at least once in five years—if elections were to be held just once, then the people providing leadership would have sought riddance of those who put their money on race horses, scoundrels and all anti-social elements. But this can never happen because elections are held every five years and occasionally there are mid-term polls as well.

HELPLESSNESS OF THE VOTERS DURING ELECTIONS

You can say that our voters too are pivotal to a proper functioning of our democratic system as it is they who go on to elect the right or the wrong candidate to the positions of leadership. Having said so, it has created a sort of helplessness for the voters as all parties and leaders are birds of the same feather. A political leader who wins elections through unfair means, treachery, theft, etc., cannot be the owner of a self-respecting, ethical personality. The emotional expanse of such people would be limited to, at the most, their party only, an unstable expansion for their own party—and that too only when the interests of the leaders are vested in that particular party only.

Those people in our country who fight and win elections through unfair means and incur expenses of lacs and crores, in whatever post they are, should accept that they are people of confined and limited spheres. Wherever these emotionally confined people provide leadership from, they spread corruption and create an atmosphere (this is the natural human law that the emotional sphere of people who submit meekly to such leadership also gets confined) where immorality spreads like plague throughout the society.

PEOPLE WITH A NARROW EMOTIONAL SPHERE SHOULD BE REMOVED FROM BIG RESPONSIBILITIES

The people who acquire leadership posts but continue to live in a very narrow emotional sphere of 'I' and 'My', never shy away from begging or becoming a race horse or evading their duties. Where there is no emotional attachment there is no turning back from doing anything absurd or nonsensical. Rather the narrow or limited emotional sphered people that is, people of 'I' and 'My', are manipulating to gain more and more money, respect and love, by grabbing the leadership positions which is the biggest source of getting money and recognition.

Such narrow-sphered leaders can be divided into two categories—one, those who are totally corrupt and indulge in nefarious activities openly and shamelessly, the other is of those who are not so low or immoral as to exhibit their immorality so brazenly. In fact these people are the white-collared immoral people who ostensibly appear to say or do the right things but behind the curtain, are busy in their own personal gains and satisfaction through money, respect and love to satisfy the 'I' of their narrow sphere.

In total contrast to the above two, is the category of those people who possess a large emotional sphere with moral values, who are dedicated to the cause of the nation and the society with a true sense of honesty.

A small thought may be popping up in your head as to where the present leaders get love and respect from? In fact, people of a very narrow sphere are capable of generating love and respect owing to their designation and status. The reason is that the common man out of ignorance can recognize people only by their designation or external personality and that is related to the material and the (status) authority. So, the so-called leaders are always busy in acquiring food for their external personality, however hollow their internal personality may be. Such people always live in excessive tension about getting richer. They recognize and understand only the food for their external personality. Their condition is like that of a dentist watching a boxing bout, who is sometimes cheering one boxer and sometimes his opponent. When asked why he was supporting both, he says that he stands to gain either ways, regardless of which of the two loses his teeth.

Well I don't want to generalize my statement. There are political leaders, mainly from the senior bracket, who are above board and are definitely having a large emotional sphere and they want to think and do good for the society and the country. But they are in minority, hence are helpless under the majority of people who exist in a confined or a limited emotional sphere.

There should, I repeat, be a very strict system where even knowledgeable, intelligent leaders in politics, administration or judiciary or education or media or large corporate houses with confined emotional sphere should either not be selected at all or if selected and recognized later as having a confined emotional sphere, should definitely be removed from big responsibilities.

We, in Sahara follow it very strictly. We strongly believe that a person who is highly qualified, knowledgeable with high intelligence but without the right human qualities or character meaning thereby, having a confined emotional sphere, has no place in our family, especially in the case of a senior person. We remove and replace them with the right human beings, who may be less qualified, less knowledgeable and less intelligent but who possess a large emotional sphere. They are the ones who engage the right talents and go on to produce very good results.

Of course, my experience says that continuous teaching on life changes people drastically though everyone takes time to change his or her polluted, defective nature (sub-conscious reflexes).

All humans have positive and negative characteristics, we are born with them, we live with them and we die with them too. But it has always been seen that if proper education of life is given and a proper, positive and a non-discriminatory human environment is created, most of the people then desire to act, react positively and in all expressions are dominated by positive characteristics.

So I emphatically and repeatedly say that strict selection, education, examination, accountability and then continuous teachings are a must, indeed a must for those who are occupying positions of leadership in various activities and work spheres.

The people who are within the emotional sphere of 'My', that is limited to the welfare of their immediate family members, are generally decent people. They are not negative for the society. But to provide leadership in the realm of bureaucracy, media, corporate and all kinds of political streams, such people who are in the sphere of 'My' that is limited to their immediate family, shall only have the welfare and prosperity of their immediate family members as their priority. Well, anybody and everybody will have a natural desire to look after their family members but the first priority should never be that. I want to make it clear once again that if somebody's emotional sphere is confined to 'I', his first priority will always be his own needs, desires or greed; if the sphere is of 'My', then it will be towards his self and his immediate family members; if the sphere is of 'We', then it will be towards his work place; if the sphere is of 'We All', it will be the society and the nation and if the sphere is of 'Us', it will be towards the entire mankind.

Proper self-motivation is generated through proper continuous teaching and maintaining checks. Thus, good quality, balanced people whose sphere extends to 'My' and 'We', can always be convinced to shift their priority sphere to 'We All' and 'Us'.

IMPROVEMENT IN THE ELECTORAL SYSTEM IS THE SOLUTION

To a certain extent it is correct to say that in our country, corruption has spread even to the labour class and among people doing big and small jobs, in fact the entire masses. But the most important question is, who is to be held guilty—the masses or the people providing leadership. The entire fault is of the people providing leadership. After all, water flows from above to reach the bottom. If the water above is clear at its source, then the stream that originates from the source and gushes forth will also be comparatively clear when it reaches the bottom. However, if the water is contaminated, then the dirt at the top will pollute the stream that reaches the bottom.

CURB ON EXPENSES DURING ELECTIONS IS A MUST

On priority it is essential that the area providing leadership should be improved upon. For this, there should be improvements in the electoral system, curb on the misuse of expenses, means to alleviate the feeling of insecurity in the area of leadership and in this way, the paths of non-corruptible people be cleared. When people with an expanded emotional sphere and those who believe in national interests being paramount, occupy the position of leadership, only then would our democracy become a democracy in the true sense and prove beneficial to the cause of the masses.

After knowing all this you will agree that the one direct way to rise above such an alarming situation, so as to acquire a state of excellence is to reduce the election expenses to a minimum. For this, the government in every constituency should make available a fixed spacious ground with the arrangements of mike, tent etc. Whatever a candidate has to speak about, should be from a stipulated place and at a stipulated time. Their statements should be published lawfully, in the right proportion, by the local newspapers. Candidates should be permitted the use of only two or three vehicles. More than two-three vehicles should be strictly prohibited. Posters and banners should be prohibited, instead black and white handbills of one or two pages in pre-decided quantities, should be printed and distributed, that too by the candidates themselves.

The media should play a justifiable role here and it should be made mandatory for all local newspapers/channels to continuously carry the statements of the candidates in the electoral fray. Of course, the space and the frequency of news coverage should be fixed and provided in equal measure to five major candidates; for the other candidates, the space and frequency could be even lesser.

By adopting these measures the election expenses can be

brought down considerably.

As of today, the matter of drastically curtailing the election expenses will sound somewhat illogical, especially for those who are into the political mainstream. But to those people, whose emotions are associated with the nation and society, the matter of reduction in elections expenses will not sound illogical or out of place, instead they will institute a constructive revolution for such a system to be in place.

Yes, people with confined spheres, politicians with unethical values will definitely not want a system that advocates a significant lowering in such expenses as that will not allow them to procure anti-social elements, weapons or arms. But after some days, the influence of the external personalities of such people will fade away—they will vanish into oblivion and then good people with expanded spheres will start coming in. Thus, our beloved nation will once again become so strong and beautiful that it will emerge as the best in the world.

A NEW CONCEPT: "NOMINATED DEPUTY MEMBER OF PARLIAMENT (NDMP)" IN THE LOWER HOUSE [LOK SABHA]

Having discussed a critical issue at length, I would like to share with you a thought that has often crossed my mind.

As representatives of their electorates and being a part of a Parliamentary democracy, Members of the Parliament

[MPs] are responsible primarily towards the people of their own constituency, then towards the state they represent and consequently, the overall well-being of the nation.

As a Parliamentary norm, it is obligatory on the part of MPs to meet up with their electorates and try to gauge their aspirations, take note of their grievances, through regular visits to their respective constituencies. But often out of their own compulsions, arising out of personal or professional commitments as part of the social elite and occupying posts of considerable eminence in addition to their roles as Parliamentarians, they are unable to visit their constituencies as often as they would desire. This often brings into question their ideals and commitment towards their constituencies and the people whom they have come to represent.

I therefore, suggest that for overall betterment in the performance of MPs and improved coordination between an MP and his constituency, a new law be enacted through the Parliament.

As per the law, a new post of **Nominated Deputy Member of Parliament (NDMP)** would be created in the Lower House (Lok Sabha) and the person nominated as such, shall be attached with each of the elected Members of Parliament.

The NDMP will have full authority on behalf of the Member of Parliament to serve in the overall interest of country without being directly involved in the day-to-day political affairs.

The elected MPs can send NDMPs to attend the Parliament sessions on their behalf. Of course, it would not be practical for both the MPs and their NDMPs to attend the Parliament sessions together owing to the limited seating capacity of the Parliament House. But if a particular MP is allocated a specific time and date to make a speech or to discuss an important point in the Parliament, then on such occasions, the NDMP can be allowed to attend the Parliament session along with his senior MP.

The NDMP will have to do a lot of creative thinking, planning and then concentrate on executing them suitably towards the development of the constituencies on behalf of his senior MP, thereby, towards the country's overall uplift and progress.

NDMPs shall also concentrate towards maintaining perfect law and order, taking care of genuine grievances of people of the constituency and also safeguarding against anybody indulging in undue favoritism, discrimination, injustice or corruption in the constituency. The main purpose of this would be to control the people in the government machinery and also those who are elected at the local or district level.

The MPs and NDMPs shall be empowered to select or nominate 3 persons, one of whom at the most could be from the political stream. These 3 persons shall always be based at the constituency and regularly listen to the grievances of the people to try and resolve them. These 3 persons shall also be government appointed/nominated persons and shall be given full authority to function on behalf of the respective MPs and NDMPs. At any point of time, the MPs and NDMPs can remove or replace these 3 persons if their work is not found to be satisfactory. But essentially such action can only be taken with the consent and signatures of both the MPs and NDMPs.

As regards the perks and other benefits, the NDMP and the 3 persons (who can be jointly addressed as **Constituency Caretakers** or **CCTs** for brief or by some other appropriate Hindi name) should be given suitable remuneration along with a chauffer-driven vehicle with fuel. They should be allowed all travel, telephone-related expenses, etc. Never should they face up to financial strain, rather they should feel that financially they are being well looked after.

NDMPs and CCTs shall not be under any compulsion to give up on their current occupations, they would in fact, be allowed to continue with their own professions, businesses, etc., alongside carrying out their newly assigned roles.

If the selection process is fair and proper, we shall have the right personalities occupying these posts, who shall comfortably take care of all the responsibilities assigned to them. If they are not allowed to continue with their own work where they are already quite successful in conjunction with their newly assigned responsibilities, then the ones who come to serve at these positions will only be failed, unskilled and potentially weak, bad characters, which is not the objective of this thought at all.

We should select people with an absolutely clean character, not having an iota of criminal background. They must be well qualified, educated, good and cultured human beings. They may be recently retired judges, senior and reputed advocates, retired personnel from the Armed forces etc., service-oriented professionals, teachers, chartered accountants, business persons, engineers, doctors etc. (during the selection process, only the best quality personalities should be selected and two out of the selected three should positively be non-political.)

There shall be Central Sub-committees, Committees led by the Hon'ble Prime Minister who shall select NDMPs and who can also remove or replace them on any charges or owing to incompetence during the service tenure. The MPs themselves cannot remove or replace the NDMPs. They can, of course, approach the Hon'ble Prime Minister's Committees if they want their NDMPs to be removed or replaced.

All Members of Parliament in the Lower House are elected by groups of citizens of the country regardless of the kind of electoral system under which they are selected and it becomes their prime duty to maintain peace and communal harmony among the people of their respective constituencies. Yet all kinds of confusions prevail in political parties in respect of religion, caste, creed and due to so many other complexities and equations, which I do not want to elaborate upon here. I do not think such things should be mentioned aloud. These are delicately sensitive matters that can be taken care of at an appropriate stage. What I do want to say is that the percentage of bad quality population has increased considerably, so whoever gets a majority of votes may not always be the right and deserving person for the society.

And our most Adorable Prime Minister, Hon'ble Shri Narendra Modi Saahab always speaks of good governance, so good governance should be seen in all sectors, areas and levels, keeping in view the HUGE size of our country.

Important—If we think of taking this concept forward and if I am asked to explain further, I shall try to elaborate with micro-level details and definitions.

Population

In the times to come, there will be a dramatic decrease in the number of talented, intelligent, educated and cultured people with the right values, which will have a negative bearing on our democratic set up. Persons leading a bestial life will outnumber others and play a decisive political role. All this is leading to a very unfortunate and menacing situation.

2. Population

Population explosion is not only a problem in India; it has reached menacing proportions all over the world, especially in the poorer countries. In a developing country like India, the rapid speed of growing population has put intense pressure on our system and overall development. Hence, the first and foremost responsibility of the country is to control population.

What factors-political, economic, social and religious—favour our current efforts to reduce India's birth rate? The foremost is an awareness that population growth is the nation's number one problem, both at the government and non-government levels.

Programmes like family planning are being implemented and married couples are being directed not to produce more than two children. But it is our misfortune that the direction of our population policy has now gone in the reverse. Those well-to-do people who have the resources to provide education to scores of children and the capacity to make them able citizens are having just two children while those who do not have adequate facilities to bring up their children are giving birth to ten children. Amongst these, none becomes an able citizen.

Thus, in matters of population the country is suffering on the counts of quantity and quality both. Quality is going down, even as the population is going up. Hence, it is essential to think deeply on the population policy. Such policies are the need of the hour as which control population and develop quality in a human being.

At the time of Independence, our country's total population stood at around 36 crore. According to a UN Estimate, it has now touched 1.33 billion (133 crore), which makes us the second most populous country in the world after China and a large segment of this population is condemned to an extremely poor quality life.

The study reveals that India represents almost 17.84% of the world's population (which has crossed the 7 billion mark), even though it accounts for just 2.4% of total land area of the globe, which is around 135.79 million sq. km. This means one out of six people on this planet earth lives in India. Every year India adds more people than any other country in the world-about 18 million, much larger than about 7 million in China.

By the end of 2030, India is predicted to have more than 1.53 billion people, making it the most populous nation in the world, if the current trends are maintained.

HORRIFYING SCENARIO OF OUR POPULATION

Approximately 70,000 children are born every day in the country, almost one every 1.25 seconds. One-third of them weigh half the weight of a normal healthy child. According to government statistics, the country has about 6,50,000 primary schools. But the alarmingly high birth rate requires the additional establishment of 1 lac. primary schools every year. This is an impossible proposition. Where other countries of the world have one doctor for every 50 persons, India has one doctor for every 2,000 people.

Moreover, a majority of our population still remains unskilled, with about 26% of it lying below the poverty line, which has become an obstacle towards our sustainable economic development, as we are unable to utilize our human resource to the optimum.

WRONG POLICIES AGGRAVATE THE PROBLEM

Until now, there has been only lip service to the cause of population control. As things stand today, the number of well meaning and conscientious and cultured persons is fast declining. On the other hand, the number of persons leading a pathetic existence is on the rise with no signs of this condition improving in the near future. In this respect, family planning has played a negative role. I understand this from my personal experience.

When my second child was born, the doctor asked me if I would like to opt for a family-planning operation on my wife. I immediately gave my consent.

I recall that I was given a certificate and gifts by the government in Gorakhpur. I was very happy. At that point in time I considered myself a true patriot who had done something good for the country by following the two-child norm. But when I look back I realize that out of ignorance I probably committed an unpatriotic act. I will explain why.

Even if I had produced 10 children, I would have given those many good citizens to the country because God has given me the financial and social capability to do so. (But it does not justify that a capable and well-off person should produce 10 children). We stopped at two but on the other hand, around 10 children are being born to single parents on the roads and in slums.

THE NEGATIVE ROLE OF PEOPLE LEADING AN ANIMAL-LIKE EXISTENCE

The family planning program which has been in force for the past several decades, makes for a sad story.

India started taking measures to curtail the population growth rate quite early. In fact India launched the National Family Planning Program as early as the 1950s and became the first country in the world to have a planned population policy.

The family planning program did yield some noticeable results and brought down the nation's fertility rate quite significantly. But with the efficiency of the administrative machinery of the various state governments not being uniform, there were variations in the achievement of family-planning targets over a longer run. Thus, the efforts by and large failed to attain the ultimate goal and the population of India since we gained independence in 1947, has risen dramatically.

Here I would like to underline the difference between a human and an animal. Like humans, animals need water, air and food, produce offspring and have emotions too. But an animal does not have proper thinking power whereas a human is known as the most superior among all living creatures only because he can think. But, if this specific faculty (thinking) of a human is not noble, is destructive, and not disciplined, then he degenerates to the state of an animal. In such a case, an animal is far better than such a human as an animal does less harm and causes lesser troubles. Unfortunately, the number of persons with such vulgar and narrow-minded tendencies is growing in enormous proportions.

Ours is a democratic set-up, which is based on the rule of the majority. The elected representatives run the government. But recent years have seen an increase in the number of leaders who have unhealthy, animal-like tendencies.

Sense of security is a human being's prime concern,

therefore, a degenerated man chooses a person with a similar mindset to be his leader. Unfortunately, the number of such fraudulent leaders is rising rapidly. It will, in turn, lead to a dramatic decrease in the number of talented, intelligent, educated and cultured people with the right values, which will have a negative bearing on our democratic set up. Persons leading a bestial life will outnumber others and play a decisive political role.

All this is leading to a very unfortunate and menacing situation. Truly speaking, the growth of a population with poor quality is our real problem, not the quantitative or numerical growth of population, with poverty, illiteracy, unhygienic living and a high fertility rate being the major contributory factors.

INDIA COULD HAVE BEEN A PROSPEROUS NATION IF...

Try to imagine, if India had one-third of its present population, it would have been the most beautiful, the richest and the most prosperous country in the world.

While studying population, I found that people often talk of developed countries but they don't take into consideration the fact that the US population is one-third that of ours even though it has a four-times larger land area. Of course, while saying so I have taken into account that the entire land mass in the US is not habitable. Still the contrast makes for a startling disclosure. The US has 18 persons living in one square kilometer, whereas in urban India as many as 7,000 people are cramped in the same space. So there is no reason why the US should not be a developed country.

A SICK MENTALITY

In fact, those living in slums tend to produce more children under the false assumption that it will provide them with more earning hands in old age. But this thinking stems from their sense of insecurity with regard to the future. They tend to think that fewer children mean lesser earning for them in which case they will find it difficult to make both ends meet. Therefore, we as a nation, particularly the government should make all-out efforts so that the people belonging to the weaker sections do not suffer from a sense of financial insecurity about the future, if they produce fewer children. If these efforts were to succeed, then the qualitative growth of the population would not come down and neither would quality population be reduced to a minority as it appears to be the case now.

Our population is flourishing on poor qualifications and low merits. It means we are being defeated in terms of qualitative workforce. This is the biggest reason for our downfall. I was asked if there was any solution. I said 'It is really very simple.

Self-interest or 'I' in a man is a very dominant trait. There is a need to understand man's needs and aspirations and find ways and means to fulfill them'.

AN IDEAL FAMILY AND THE BENEFITS THAT CAN BE PROVIDED TO THEM AS A WAY OF ENCOURAGEMENT

First of all, we need to finalise the definition of an "ideal family".

Those who have one or two children, as they do in the People's Republic of China, would fall under the category of an ideal family and this should be passed as law by the Parliament. Such of those families which qualify as 'ideal' families can then be provided with a host of attractive amenities and facilities.

But families which have more than 2 children should be excluded from the ambit of an ideal family.

To all of those who fall within the periphery of an ideal family, the following benefits could be extended:

1. IF PROPER SECURITY FOR OLDER PEOPLE CAN BE ENSURED, ALONG WITH OLD AGE PENSION THE TENDENCY TO HAVE LARGER FAMILIES CAN BE CONTAINED. THUS TO ENCOURAGE THE IDEAL FAMILY CONCEPT, OLD AGE PENSION SCHEME SHOULD NOT BE LIMITED TO GOVERNMENT PLANS ONLY.

PRIVATE CORPORATE SECTOR MUST ALSO BE INVOLVED IN THIS.

2. Renowned industrial houses have shown interest in providing old age security subject to the fact that they get some tax benefits on the money spent on such programmes. The current laws governing taxation can make a provision to allow for this benefit.

3. I would even go so far as to say that to ensure adequate help to senior citizens, a special tax must be imposed on those who are having substantial income.

4. Families that commit to being an ideal family should be extended all facilities for child-birth, right from the conception till the time of delivery of the child.

5. When the children of ideal families grow up they should be given the privilege of proper education along with priority in higher and professional education consisting of engineering, management and other job-oriented courses.

6. They should also have their jobs secured, or else, should be given the highest priority for jobs, both in public and private sector enterprises.

7. The ideal families should have the privilege of reservation with important posts in governmental vocations, such as in police, administrative, judicial services and specifically, all responsibilities and opportunities in the political

sphere. Such privileges can also extend to promotions.

8. Any kind of loan facility in big and small businesses should be extended to encourage the ideal family concept.

9. The ideal families must also be encouraged by being provided a relaxation in the interest rates in governmental/ non-governmental loans and should be entitled to government subsidies too, besides scholarships and other financial help to the children.

10. In the same way, in the disposal of court cases, ideal families should be given precedence over others, whenever possible.

11. There must be legal provision so that they may avail of all other small-big aides and facilities etc., of life that are necessary, from governmental or any other reliable source.

12. The law must also provide for maximum facility to the economically backward ideal families, who should have more reservations in jobs as compared to economically advanced ideal families. But despite the variance, the said privileges would be extended to both the classes so long as they fall into the category of an ideal family.

13. Ideal families should also get medical incentives including the provision of surgical procedures, treatment and medical check-ups at discounted rates.

14. Ideal Indian families should get the benefits of all

government controlled facilities like rail/air/bus fare, hotel accommodation, entrance form fees etc., with attractive discounts.

15. They may be provided life insurance coverage on preferential basis.

16. A majority of our population resides in the rural belts. Therefore, infrastructural development in rural areas is important as it generates employment and helps in curbing population growth (as was done in China). Ideal families identified in the rural areas must be given direct access to land, water, forest and other resource materials on priority.

17. Such of these families may also be given significant privileges like interest-free loan for acquiring fertilizers, tractors and other agricultural machinery like the latest equipment, utilities and irrigation systems, besides fuel subsidy and/or any other requirement on preferential basis.

18. In India, land related programmes such as land reforms, land consolidation, land redistribution, land reclamation, land development etc., were carried out but were never associated with family planning. Whatever be the land activities conducted, a fair share of the benefits that accrue thereof, should go to the ideal families.

19. Under the land acquisition policy, tenants and landless

farm labour are the worst sufferers. Programmes should be devised and conducted in such a way that no one is uprooted from their native place and resources towards a secure livelihood are made available to them. In this regard, the ideal families must be given priority.

20. In land distribution system that still needs to be carried out in a big way, ideal families should be given priority. Towards this, they could either be given ownership of a cultivable piece of land or their contract of work should be made binding and obligatory so that their livelihood is secure.

21. The planned implementation of a **'land consolidation'** programme can bring in substantial social benefits and the same could be extended to ideal families by way of efficient and sustainable use of land resources and promoting their equitable distribution.

22. The ideal families would benefit from a land consolidation programme that aims to build upon fragmented and under-utilised land or land damaged by natural or mining disasters, and develop unused land resources to increase overall productivity.

23. Land consolidation can lead to improvements in agriculture. Allowing the segment of our farmer's fraternity that falls within the ambit of an ideal family, to acquire farms with fewer parcels that are larger and

better shaped, and to expand the size of their holdings would enable them to become more competitive.

24. Improving the tenure structure can facilitate the adoption of new agricultural technologies by the farmers leading to a more prosperous and efficient agricultural sector. Rationalising the tenure structure can facilitate environmental protection and also support the farmers with better land use planning and land management.

25. The members of ideal families may be given priority based employment in all land development activities in the rural areas.

26. Land consolidation can promote social stability among ideal families by increasing the number of new jobs created which in turn will lead to increase in tax yields, a trend already visible in Western Europe.

27. Also, there could be 'compensatory benefits' to the ideal families through the implementation of a rural land consolidation plan which may include : access to motor vehicles to all farms with better communication systems, faster transport of agricultural products, improved conditions for agricultural holdings, increased agricultural income due to major reduction in production cost, among others.

28. Presently, corporate farming is in the offing. Wherever

it takes place, ideal families may be given priority in the employment opportunities generated by such farming.

If we can manage to strictly implement these rules and regulations over all those families which fall under the definition of two children ideal family, I firmly believe that we can enrich our lives as well as the life of the nation.

One more important issue to be tackled is that the poor and the downtrodden do not have a source of entertainment which is most important in human life as food for internal personality. In other words, entertainment is one's emotional food and so is sex. We must extend help to every 'mohalla' [locality] in the country, where cheap-priced condoms could be made available and easily purchased by all, even from a betel shop in their 'mohallas'. After doing this, I don't think family planning activity would be required at all.

NOTHING CAN BE ACHIEVED IN THE ABSENCE OF STRINGENT LAWS

The legislation on population control must provide for stringent measures (with some kind of punishment if necessary) against those parents who are thought of as dishonouring the ideal family norm.

Besides not being extended economic benefits/privileges

by the government, I strongly suggest that the parents of all those either not living in an ideal family ambit or violating the spirit of such a family should not be allowed to vote i.e. should be disenfranchised and should not be allowed to stand as candidates during any election. This may apply to all offices from the President to 'Panchayat' level. They may not be allowed access to a ration card or a passport either. If possible, the child exceeding the ideal family norm should also be deprived of the right to vote. THIS MAY APPEAR HARSH BUT WILL BE EXTREMELY GOOD AND HIGHLY DESIRABLE FOR A HEALTHY DEMOCRACY.

An experts' committee can be formed to give a final shape to these legal provisions. The law should be implemented only after one year of its enactment. This intervening one-year duration can be termed as warning period during which all parents must realize the perils of transgressing the ideal family norm.

AN APPEAL

I call upon all the well informed people of my country, especially those associated with mass communication, to take the initiative, find solutions, and guide the nation. They should ascertain that all the people of this country follow suit and launch a massive nationwide constructive movement. I know that you will face many difficulties in accomplishing this task. People will try to discourage you but you should have the will to carry on with zeal and fervor.

If we don't stop the rapid growth of our country's bad quality population, and this situation continues for another few years, then all pavements, roads will be filled with a class of people that is of a weak and bad quality constituting the unemployed 'have-nots'—and a situation of a civil war would soon erupt.

This alarming situation will not be visible at the same time countrywide and neither will it arise all of a sudden. Things will deteriorate as a gradual course from one area to another, from one state to another before this becomes an irreversible trend all across the country.

IT IS HIGH TIME [IN FACT WE ARE ALREADY QUITE LATE] THAT THIS MOST IMPORTANT AND HIGHLY CRITICAL ISSUE OF OUR COUNTRY WAS TAKEN CARE OF WITH UTMOST SERIOUSNESS BY THE GOVERNMENT.

Education System

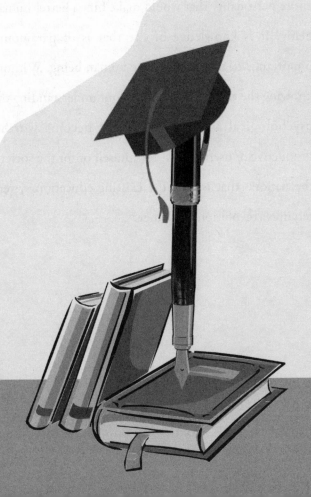

In schools and colleges, we attain a level of literacy on a particular subject but are not educated there in the real sense. Being educated implies the development of one's entire personality that would make him a better human being. It is knowledge of life that is of paramount importance to make one a true human being. Without knowing the truths of life or without understanding the psychological aspects one cannot become worthy, productive or useful either for himself or for the society, the nation. That is why the existing education system requires a revolutionary change.

3. Education System

A sad reality of today's education system is that though it is correct from the perspective of imparting work-oriented skills, that is in generating the ability to earn one's livelihood and to get a job, is not adequate in imparting true knowledge.

IN SCHOOLS AND COLLEGES, WE ATTAIN A LEVEL OF LITERACY BUT ARE NOT REALLY EDUCATED THERE

In schools and colleges in the present times, we attain a level of literacy on a particular subject but are not educated there in the real sense. Being educated implies the development of one's entire personality that would make him a better human being. It is knowledge of life that is of paramount importance to make one a true human being. Without knowing the truths of life or without understanding the psychological aspects one cannot become worthy, productive or useful either for himself or for the society, the nation. That is why the existing education system requires a revolutionary change.

We need an education system that can impart all aspects

of the knowledge of life to a person and help him evolve as a true and an honest human being, whose life shows the way to the society, whose life is beautiful, whose life is useful for the nation. And it is not impossible for this to happen, it is quite possible. What is required is knowledge that is useful for life and education. (*With regard to 'Knowledge of Life', I have discussed it in detail in my earlier book 'Life Mantras'.*)

THE CURRENT EDUCATION SYSTEM NEEDS ADEQUATE REFORMS

Now, through this discourse, in national interest, I would like to appeal to the leaders of my country with folded hands that they, after careful consideration, give serious thought to bringing about the necessary reforms in our education system at the earliest, which is vital for the present as well as the future generations. Else, if the present half-baked education system continues, the coming generations will never forgive us. However much they condemn us, it will fall short of our crime. We must know why this alarming situation has arisen.

Our population density is very, very high and demands that the human aspect, the human psychology is given top priority in education.

WORK FIELD AND EDUCATION SYSTEM

Let me state that by merely acquiring the knowledge of work field or profession, the purpose of acquiring the education of life cannot be achieved. In its real sense education is that which brings about an all-round and wholesome development of our personality, so that we in turn, bring about positive and beautiful changes in our society. The education and the education system in which all-round development of personality is not possible and which does not prevent disturbing tendencies in the society, is never complete.

In ancient times the 'Gurukul' system of education was pragmatic in many respects. The priority was to infuse the students with the knowledge of life. Their personality was developed in a wholesome manner. Yet history shows that in this ancient system of education one big flaw was markedly visible that education was not available to all and sundry. It was available only to those who came from the elite ruling class or were destined to rule the state. However, at least one thing was remarkable, that it was an effective education system for the leadership clan. To lead means to shoulder the responsibility of a guardian i.e. to be a teacher for the society. A good teacher is the one who himself is well taught.

The original education system of our country was terribly affected during the Mughal Period, and the British period. They formulated the education system afresh with a view to generate blind supporters. They needed clerks and not administrators, and the education system was planned on those lines.

We are concentrating and progressing well with regard to literacy but not education [that too, mainly in the urban segment of the society]. We have to understand, take this issue very seriously.

THE EDUCATION SYSTEM AFTER INDEPENDENCE

The biggest mistake was committed after Independence. After hundreds of years of slavery it was imperative that the education system be overhauled on priority. But it never happened. And you will see that at that point in time the position of a teacher was looked down upon as being an inferior one. When an aspirant failed to become an IAS, IPS, Doctor, Engineer, Lawyer or an accountant, only then did he try to draw some solace by becoming a teacher. Until a few years ago, a parent looked at a teacher as a prospective groom for his daughter only when all his efforts to get a better groom for his daughter had failed.

HOW DOES ONE IMPROVE THE OVERALL STANDARDS OF EDUCATION?

In fact, during those times a teacher's salary and his esteem should have been the highest in the society, and for that the best selection system was needed then. The best people should have been inducted in this profession. Had this happened, the conditions in this country would have been far better. Even today things are not in the most desirable shape. It really surprises me when I find all responsible people associated with education harping on the same note, that to improve the standards of education, more and more new schools should be opened, school buildings should be renovated, more desks and benches should be fitted in the class rooms, etc.

I do agree that the opening of more schools is necessary because only then would education reach the maximum number of people. But first of all, we have to know what, after all, is education. What kind of education is to be imparted? While defining education, the first thing that comes to mind is that education means gaining knowledge. The more the education the better the life is. But only gaining knowledge of the work sector or of a particular profession cannot be termed as gaining complete knowledge.

I will repeat, with the present syllabus in schools and colleges we attain literacy but are not educated. Education is the ultimate and the most important requirement of life.

We are becoming literate but we need to be educated and as I have said in the beginning, we need to gain insight to the Education of Life.

RELIGIOUS EPICS HAVE BECOME OBJECTS OF WORSHIP WITH THE DEVELOPMENT OF THE LOGICAL MUSCLE

Another offshoot of the faulty and incomplete education system is proving to be dangerous to the society. Just like with regular physical exercise the physical muscle gets toned, by continuous practice of reading and writing the mental power emerges stronger as the logical muscle gets toned, thereby generating a strong faculty of argument.

As mentioned, in the olden days people were not so literate. Only a few people had the reach to education, hence their logical muscle and thereby, the faculty of argument was not developed all that much. The people benefited by following the values, ethics and teachings given in religious books that told them what they should and should not do.

But owing to the increased faculty of argument through the development of the logical muscle, the beautiful and wisdom-containing religious scriptures no longer suit the argumentative and logical characteristics of the educated people of modern times and thus, have gradually turned objects of ritual worship. Along with 'dos' and 'don'ts' if these books also taught as to why one should do something and why one should not, then the learner may grasp it more clearly.

So long as a man does not comprehend the reason and logic behind a matter being taught, he remains unable to adopt it in practical life; since the 'I' in a man is very powerful he does not accept a thing without weighing its pros and cons. And if he blindly adopts something, he generally does not benefit from it. Today in the society it is seen that whenever people adopt things blindly in the name of knowledge or out of a fear of religion; they gain no knowledge in the real sense of the word.

Here I quote the 'Gita' where it has been said—'Do your duty, never think of the result'. It is very much true, but when in the modern era people think about it with logic, they ask themselves, 'why should I not think of the fruits or the result ?' They want the fruits of their efforts. It is not possible for a man just to work and not to think of its fruits. So these kinds of sermons need a logical, reasonable and detailed explanation.

OUR EPICS SHOULD BE RE-EXPLAINED IN A MODERN-DAY CONTEXT

As I have explained, in schools and colleges we attain literacy but not education. Literacy only gives you a job but not a level of competence. Literacy ['saksharta'] and Education ['shiksha'] are two different subjects.

Ancient concepts prevalent in any culture have always influenced the development of knowledge and the same applies to the epics. There are many recent books which explain or interpret a number of epics in a modern context, which help unravel the richness and the wholesomeness of ancient Indian literature and its potential to enrich our knowledge base.

Such epics or scriptures which were written during the ancient times need to be re-explained in a modern-day context because as I had said earlier, with the gradual development of one's logical muscle, a human being has developed the faculty to think and analyse things, to look at things from a different perspective.

We need to encourage such books that re-look such epics from a new perspective and give greater clarity of thought. To develop more clarity, the enhancement of one's basic thought-process is essential. This will give replies to all questions attached with the main message hidden in the epics and thus, make them more acceptable and adaptable in the current-day perspective.

I feel that to educate young people in the matters of life, the psychological or the emotional aspects of life, in other words the entire philosophy of life, such books should be introduced compulsorily in their curriculum from the 10th standard itself.

While doing so, we shall not touch the original epics at all. In deciphering the multi-faceted nature of ancient Indian texts, we shall be able to gauge their importance in a modern-day perspective and their usefulness in the current educational system. The 'Gita' for example embodies 'Universal Truth'. While re-interpreting it, we shall not touch upon its core essence but only bring out its message in context of the moral and spiritual growth of mankind.

Likewise, if we follow the same pattern with regard to the other scriptures, we shall be able to comprehend in depth, the vast knowledge and wisdom contained in them, to apply it in a variety of situations in our current-day lives.

EDUCATION SHOULD HAVE A MUCH GREATER REACH

Another worrisome aspect of education or literacy is the lack of good quality teachers. According to an estimate, India is short of 12 lac teachers to provide quality education at the primary level, based on the fact that there is a requirement of one teacher for every 30 students.

This problem can be overcome by developing an on-line system of education through IT so that a battery of good teachers sitting at one place are able to reach out to millions of students in classrooms which have the facility of an electronic screen. In these classes, the local teachers would also be present as that would help them gradually enhance their faculty of good teaching.

My rough estimate/calculation is that by spending just a lac of rupees, a wonderful system such as this can be developed for a single set-up and a high standard of education can extend to the remotest corners of India.

The government can also explore the option of adding this

to the CSR [Corporate Social Responsibility] of various business houses by offering them tax benefits/rebates in return.

IN CONCLUSION .

As I have said, the impact of quality education can be felt by introducing the necessary reforms to improve its overall standard and extending its reach to the farthest corners of India.

Today we find that the society is ridden with mutual discord, disharmony, extreme tension and corruption, the reason being that the public at large is not able to receive adequate knowledge about life. Better a person's knowledge about life's philosophy, more expansive will be the development of his internal personality [or the spiritual personality] and more will be the respect, love and security that he receives. Without knowing the truths of life, without feeling and adopting them, the development of our internal personality not only goes beyond our reach but its very existence fails to stand out in a prominent manner.

This is where the role of education becomes critical not just in imparting literacy but sound knowledge of life's philosophy to students from an early age about the healthy values of life, which generate emotional satisfactions to help in the development of our internal personality and make it big. More and more of such emotional satisfactions can be had only by acquiring the knowledge of life or the philosophy of life.

In addition as I have said, we need to have a relook at our ancient Indian scriptures and epics from a current day perspective as they are the earliest form of literature that generates awareness on the eternal truths that govern the cycle of human life.

A combination of these three factors—education that imparts knowledge of life, a re-look at our ancient scriptures in a modern context and improvement in the quality standards of education that reaches out to the remotest corners—will surely regulate the education system to our national requirement and go a long way in giving us able citizens who would put the nation on the path of true and continuous progress.

Media

When the media fulfills its responsibility in a constructive way it is very useful for the society. The prime focus of media should be to promote all-round social welfare, rather than indulge in commercialism or mere sensationalizing of news. Modern print and electronic media are so rapid that any wrong information takes no time in reaching crores of readers and viewers. Hence, media's role becomes all the more significant in terms of impact on human society.

4. Media

I now would like to take up for extensive discussion the effectiveness of mass media—the most powerful instrument of communication in the current social perspective.

EFFECTIVENESS OF MEDIA

The progress of the entire human civilization is linked to the communication systems which have united the entire world. Had there been no communication among humans, neither would man have evolved nor the society, nor the nation, nor the civilization. Without media or without a communication system, we would have been unaware of our own environment and we would have been more of non-humans than human.

Through the media all things happening are communicated to everybody across the nation. When the media fulfills its responsibility in a constructive way it is very useful for the society. Unless media spreads among the common masses with proper thought, proper direction and proper education to elevate the intellectual level of people, proportionate progress in every domain of the society and the nation cannot be achieved.

The prime focus of media therefore, should be to promote all-round social welfare, rather than indulge in commercialism or mere sensationalizing of news. Modern print and electronic media are so rapid that any wrong information takes no time in reaching crores of readers and viewers. Hence, media's role becomes all the more significant in terms of impact on human society.

MEDIA IS PLAYING AN INCREASINGLY NEGATIVE ROLE

Even though media has produced miraculous transformations in the field of information, art, literature and culture, a sad reality is that it has bitterly devalued its own potential from the point of view of human interest by fostering feelings of ill-will, petty mindedness in the society.

If the role of the media remains continuously negative then the mental conditioning of the public becomes negative too, generating distrust, causing irresponsible conduct and a strong tendency to always conclude the wrong things along with indulgence in mindless criticism, etc. Such a situation removes positivism from the minds of the masses in every aspect.

In a communication system, i.e. in the media, the most significant role is that of a daily newspaper and now of the electronic media too. Media thus, plays an important role in the sustenance and preservation of the beauty of this great world. But the same media is responsible for creating narrow-mindedness and fissures in the society. Some media function in such a way as though they intend making non-humans out of humans, rather than humans out of non-humans.

THE ROLE OF A NEWSPAPER—BEFORE AND AFTER INDEPENDENCE

Publication of a newspaper is not just another business. Before Independence, publication of a newspaper was thought of as a religion or as a mission. True to its missionary ideals, media played a vital role in the on-going Independence movement, and inspired the people to live and die for their country, upholding the values of moral and ethical life as depicted in our glorious civilization and culture.

In those times newspapers fulfilled their national and social responsibilities by putting the objective of a purposeful life before the people and encouraging and inspiring their efforts to attain freedom. But the face of newspapers has altered substantially as the media itself, has undergone a drastic change in character.

If we talk of print media, those newspapers which had played an important role in securing freedom, subsequently failed to make any purposeful contribution towards sound nation-building. They should have taken an oath that they would not accord priority to material gains and hold national interest as paramount.

Media must have an understanding as to when, how much, how and what its readers need, what their social interests and what their priorities are, so that on that basis the path to their happiness, respect, peace, satisfaction and security can be ensured—not by distorting facts but by correcting the distortions; by giving priority not to sensationalise news but towards public welfare; not by neglecting the nation but by believing in nationalism as the supreme religion. Those who cannot imbibe the aforesaid truths and essentials regarding media had better not think about it. From a goods store to the iron industry, there are scores of professions (businesses) they may joyfully embrace.

The role of the media is of an elderly friend. On the one hand it keeps in mind the interests of the readers, and on the other it is mindful of the needs of the society and the nation. That simply said, means that what a reader wants and what he is to be given in the interests of the society and nation are the two things between which media should strike a balance. I feel that along with clean and healthy entertainment, media's prime job is to publish material that creates awareness on national needs.

Here again the role of the media assumes importance and the instance of negative reporting which leads to turmoil among the masses can be quoted.

NEGATIVE NEWS AND ITS IMPACT ON THE READERS

In the media world, the journalists read and write excessively hence their faculty of argument has grown very strong. They vehemently criticize the negative traits in others and very logically present them before the society. Those among the journalists who have a narrow or a limited sphere of mind, busy themselves in finding fault with people and every other organization.

There are good people in the society; good things are happening; noble deeds are being performed and creativity does manifest itself, but these narrow minded argumentative journalists never consider it logical to present such positive things.

Actually media's problem is that they are in a business and negative news sells very easily but if my journalist friends work hard to create positive stories, these too shall sell very well. But to make a positive story juicy and readable, one has to gather the 'background' maybe by sitting for hours in a library, making the write-up brief with a catchy headline [one should always write at least 3 headline options and choose the best one]. It should be divided under many sub-heads and the information should be highlighted with figures, graphs, charts etc. But to get a negative story, it just takes a few minutes [since nowadays negative stories float around every hour all the 30 days of a month].

PEOPLE BEING CONFINED TO A NARROW EMOTIONAL SPHERE OWING TO NEGATIVE NEWS

In cities if the people, particularly those who are literate, have plunged deep into the narrowness of mind, then one of the biggest reasons for this is the narrow mindedness generated by the regular reading of negative news in newspapers and in viewing news telecasts. The psychological reasons and the different aspects of people being confined to a narrow sphere can be explained through an example.

Suppose curfew is enforced in a city because of riots and people are getting injured and killed. In such a situation people, out of fear, stay inside their houses and hide in the remotest corner, whether they get food or their other needs are fulfilled or not. A human being hides in such situations because his natural sense of security of his life dominates him. In the same way when we constantly get news of rape, loot, arson, abduction, murder, dacoit raid, etc., in the morning newspapers or in the electronic media, and other frightening news items about our locality, city, society and nation, our mental sphere shrinks and the mind goes into hiding.

Our sensitivities in performing duties towards others, seeing positive qualities in them, and trusting them begin to die out. They get hidden in the narrow, emotional sphere of one's small family. In such a scenario, people lead their lives just for the sake of it and very humbly.

The decline of this sensitivity may be clearly observed in the divisive activities prevalent in the society and the country. In other words, a society with such kind of mentality and activity may be called a society of animal-like people, and the media is largely responsible for this.

Today, one perceives a sense of alienation spreading in all parts of the country. Things have come to such a pass that when a man calls out to his brother in the middle of the night, 'Wake up brother! Our neighbour's house is on fire', the immediate response of the person thus awakened is, 'You stupid, why did you wake me up? Let me sleep, you too go to bed, we anyway will read about it in tomorrow's newspapers.'

The mental (emotional) sphere of the readers is thus, continuously narrowing down owing to their reading of frightening news items on rape, murder, loot, dacoit raid etc., however, they are gradually becoming immune to such news. They need positive news, which the newspapers, electronic media should focus on.

A profusion of positive news items including due appreciation of the right people, doing good for others, for the society, for the country will help in enlarging people's emotional spheres and also will encourage them towards self-recognition and progress. Though media is also meant to check people from wrongdoings and rightly so, equally or more, we need to be positive as well, as stated above.

MEDIA-PERSONS SHOULD HAVE A FEAR OF SELF ['SWAYAMBHAY'], NOT A FEAR OF PUNISHMENT ['DANDBHAY']

Negativism in reporting degrades social virtues like love, support, fraternity and brotherhood among the masses. It also impacts collective unity, the edifice on which the entire society is founded. In this context, the role of those associated with the media becomes critical. But they can fulfil their roles only if they are fearless from within. And a person is fearless only if he has a fear of self ['swayambhay'].

Always remember that one should have a fear of one's inner-self, one's conscience as that alone would enable a person to perform his genuine duties towards others and never allow a situation to arise wherein he would need to combat his own guilt conscience. This is because a person who fears his own self will never indulge in any such work as would make him feel diminished in stature. Only the one who has a fear of self ['swayambhay'] in performing his duties towards the society, the nation, can make for a brave and fearless journalist.

I strongly believe that such people who are ethically bound and always follow their inner-self, their conscience and perform duties justifiably, strictly follow the rules, regulations, the values and teachings, never have a fear of outside punishment ['dand-bhay'] but only fear themselves, belong to a highly motivated class with a highly developed conscience level. They never get disgraced in their own esteem, instead perform their duties genuinely towards others.

SPACE CONSUMED BY NEGATIVE NEWS SHOULD NEVER BE MORE THAN THE SPACE CONSUMED BY POSITIVE NEWS

Contrary to the above, I have observed that a large number of people among the media fraternity are not guided by their inner-self, their conscience in the performance of their genuine duties towards others or in taking care of others and thus, they really need to be taken to task. It is probably out of ignorance or whatever, that a select few of my journalistic friends throughout the nation have understood and taken as their religion or birthright only to indulge in mindless criticism, which I have already explained is hugely detrimental to the interests of the society, the country, in fact, the entire mankind.

The promoters of media are largely to be blamed and very harsh punishment should be there for the offenders (for negative reporting). They should be awakened to the fact that media is purported to serve the nation and not for enjoying any special power or privilege.

As long as negative news is true, however, it may be covered suitably without being exaggerated or unduly edited but the promoters should definitely be encouraged to cover more of positive news. The maxim should be 'If you are collecting 20% of negative news, then collect 80% of positive news'. Gathering positive news means that it should project a news item appropriately and convey the right message to the readers [through print media] and the viewers and listeners [through electronic media] without, in any way, overstating the content.

WHAT KIND OF RULES SHOULD BE FRAMED?

Often individual assertions, prejudices and experiences dictate what is presented by media-persons, rather than what should ideally be. I therefore, feel that specific rules and guidelines should be framed for judging different kinds of news items, covering 3 broad categories:

- **Neutral or impartial news** which has an unbiased impact on the society, offering a versatile mix of news and information to its readers by representing both sides of a story without attempting to either take sides or to conclude which of the two is in the right. News such as these, which are objective, unbiased, non-partisan and which attempt to testify primarily to the truthfulness of events and also to treat controversial issues in a fair and dispassionate manner, are to be welcomed and need to be prioritized as such.

- **Negative news** which promotes wrongful tendencies among the masses should be curbed and not be highlighted beyond a point. By this, I do not mean we should impose censorship or outright ban over such news items, as freedom of speech is an inseparable part of our democratic framework. However, it needs to be ensured that the element of negativism is there only to the extent that it relates to the authenticity of the news. If the negativism goes further beyond and one resorts to mindless sensationalism, then he or she should be liable to the strictest form of punishment.

- **Positive news** which encourages, gives proper publicity to good deeds and makes them popular at any small or big level and over a widened sphere, needs to be promoted and disseminated. As such, media-persons should be encouraged to propagate the element of positivism in news. The benefits of those newspersons who exhibit a positive mindset and are scrupulous in the performance of their genuine duties i.e. presenting the news with positivism as its essence, should be maximized.

THE SETTING UP OF 'FAST-TRACK COURTS'

There is no denying that a strong and robust media is pivotal to the core of our democratic structure. Freedom of press and the freedom of expression form the very basis of a democratic form of government; these have been incorporated in our constitution as fundamental rights. In a democratic set-up, therefore, media should have absolute freedom but with a clear sense of responsibility and subject to certain restrictions so as to ensure that the news that is circulated does not directly or indirectly have a bad influence on the society.

But as I have explained, media often tends to come across as the worst enemy of the society. Hence, it is essential that laws are formulated so as to disallow the media from bringing about a decay in the social fabric while it pursues its own ends.

For this, special courts need to be constituted to ensure that the conduct of the media is based on absolute truth and is in accordance with sound press ethics and to try those who distort facts and tell lies in the matters of public welfare.

I feel the solution is to set up **'fast track courts'** to deal with people in the media who indulge in false, concocted reporting. This may appear unusual and, on reflection, extremely hard to implement, but at least, it shall ensure swift justice and bring the offenders to book without subjecting one to a prolonged wait.

In the true spirit of its functioning, cases can be expeditiously disposed off by a fast-track court within a given time span and those media-persons who are found to be guilty can be convicted maximum within a month or two with punishment by way of imprisonment for a minimum of two years. Then depending upon the complexity of the cases and on the extent of wrongdoing, a penalty of Rs. 10-15 crore up to a maximum of Rs. 100 crore may be imposed upon the ones who publish such negative news (in effect, on the owners of such publications).

We journalists, the publishers, the promoters of media should always keep in mind that our basic aim is to always contribute towards the greater interests of the society, the country, in fact, the entire mankind. As such, for the media to thrive amid a constructive framework, it has to be divested of such destructive, anti-social elements. And to ensure that such elements are not allowed to further debase the media and are weeded out of the system fast and quick, swift dispensation of justice will be the need of the hour.

THE CREATION OF AN 'ADVISORY BOARD' TO FACILITATE THE DECISION-MAKING OF THE 'FAST-TRACK' COURTS

One of the problems that such courts are bound to face up to is to be able to adjudicate on a particular case based on the information/facts collected within the limited time-span as it may not constitute as evidence that is strong enough to prosecute/ punish the offenders.

To address this, a board comprised of eminent members from various walks of life, like education (professors), religion, arts, bureaucracy etc., may be constituted, whose prime role will be of a 'watch-dog' dedicated to the task of keeping tabs on the overall functioning and operative efficiency of the media fraternity. In doing so, they will ensure that the guidelines as framed for the 3 kinds of news items are adhered to, in letter and spirit.

One of their prime responsibilities would be to frame rules to identify the leading lights who promote the media in a manner that basic human rights and dignity are respected and at the same time, the potential wrongdoers who manipulate the media to gain their ends.

Information which may be false, prejudicial, insulting or infringing upon one's private life or personal reputation will have to be closely examined by the Board and the person concerned should be given a reasonable time to explain his act. If the explanation is not found as satisfactory, they would be made liable to punishment.

Such a board would be linked to the 'fast-track' courts to whom, they would submit their opinion based on their findings and observations.

This would help the courts to speedily dispose off matters as they would have sufficient evidence to decide the cases on merit.

IN CONCLUSION

Finally, on this media issue, I will say:

For all of us associated in some way or the other with the media, the most beautiful truth is that India is our home, we are a family, nationality is our religion and idealism based on humanity is our philosophy. We know, collectivism is the key to a beautiful life; self-respect and dutifulness, our tradition, 'Karmayog', our nature and truth, our worship—our 'Pooja' (Hindu way of worship), 'Ibadat' (Islamic way of prayer), 'Ardaas' (Sikh way of prayer) or the Christian way of prayer.

In our organization, Sahara, it is our strong claim that in the last 39 years of our existence, never have we done anything against the law, rules or regulations (not just technically but also in the true spirit keeping in mind that there is always an important reason behind framing any law and people should abide by that), never indulged in unwanted monetary transactions, have always followed basic values, ethics. No promoter, all of whom are workers out of their work contribution, has ever taken or shall ever take any dividend or has a share in any profit/asset of the company.

IN SPITE OF EVERYTHING SAID AND DONE, MORE THAN 80% OF THE TIME OUR SAHARA PEOPLE GET TO READ OR HEAR BASELESS, CONCOCTED, NEGATIVE NEWS.

I REALLY PITY OUR MEDIA.

With a sense of pity, I would also like to say from the point of view of national interests, that many a time, the media comes up with 100% false and fabricated news, which affects the functioning of the National Administrative System and thereby, decisions already documented in government files often get changed. Based on such news reporting, files are either opened or closed—many such instances are coming out in the open and verdicts of even the Hon'ble Courts get altered.

All of those who belong to the media fraternity, must sit together and take due care of the media, with a view to national interests. Otherwise, if the nation's growth is obstructed, if there is mass failure of the systems of governance, if injustice in the society takes precedence and there is large-scale sorrow and pain, tension, fear and envy among the people, the media will be labeled—in fact, is already being labeled—as the leading offender to the cause.

As it touches almost every aspect of human life, let not media be allowed to being used as a weapon of mass destruction, instead it should function as a strong, unshakeable pillar of our noble democratic set-up.

Religion

I am of the firm opinion that the interests of the nation are paramount and should always be placed above religion and all religious beliefs. I strongly believe that to preserve and propagate the rich emotional unity of our large Indian family and reinforce the spirit of 'unity within diversity', a 'National Religion' is truly essential as it would bring about a social integration of all our religious beliefs, customs and rituals, thus providing a strong impetus to healthy and collective emotional co-existence. This would also go a long way in building a stronger, a united and a much more prosperous India.

5. Religion

WHAT IS RELIGION

A word that must be falling almost every day on your ears and appearing in all the major and minor discourses is 'religion'. If you are asked about 'religion', you might talk about worship, recitation, namaz, etc. But in truth, this is not religion. In our own country our ancestors used the word 'religion' for the word 'duty'. For example, people say—'Daily wash and purification is your religion; to take a meal is your religion; to raise your child properly is your religion; to marry off your daughter on time is your religion, and to share in the sorrows and joys of the people in your locality is your religion, etc. In Hindi, we say 'DHARMA' for the word, 'Religion'. And 'DHARMA' is Duty.

In fact, all the three—the sense of respect, the sense of religion and the sense of duty, have one and the same meaning. The more the sense of respect in a man, the better he is in performing his duties. The more a man performs his duties the more religious he is. Religion in its true sense is nothing but fulfilling one's duties towards others. Religion enriches and enhances a man's internal personality. Principles of religion instill humane traits in a man which enable him to fulfill his duties towards self as well as others.

Out of sheer ignorance people give rituals the status of religion. Rituals and other modes of worship are only practices that help people unite emotionally. Rituals bind a man to rules and regulations so that he may maintain his religion. But because rituals are adopted as religion itself, everything has gone wrong in the society causing various kinds of fissures and fragmentations. This is purely due to ignorance. Giving importance to rituals over religion is just like a person dressed in army uniform, saluting all the time and not going to battle.

RELIGION IS THE PERFORMANCE OF DUTIES AND NOT RITUALS

In this way, religion is duty and duty is religion. In this relation I recall a mythological story. Once Narad Muni went to Lord Vishnu and said to him—'O Lord, tell me who your greatest devotee in this universe is?' Narad thinks the Lord will instantly say that it is he and he alone, Narad, who chants His name 'Narayan, Narayan' all the time. Narad is almost certain that Lord Vishnu is going to say: 'It's you Narad'. But the Lord says to him—'If you want to see the greatest devotee of mine, go to the Earth. In a certain village lives a certain farmer who is my greatest devotee'.

Narad feels very bad but is curious to unravel the mystery

of this devotee farmer. So he comes down to the Earth, reaches the village and watches the farmer. The farmer rises early in the morning, attends to his cattle, milks the cows, and taking his tiffin box sets out for his fields. Whatever work he has to do he accomplishes in the fields and returns home. He goes to his neighbor's house, shares their joys and sorrows, looks after the needs of his family. Then again he attends to his cattle, chats, eats with his family members and calling it a day he says with folded hands—'O, My Lord' and retires to bed.

Narad comes back to Lord Vishnu and says—'I chant your name all my waking and sleeping hours, yet in your eyes I am not your biggest devotee, whereas the farmer who utters your name just once a day, that too when he goes to sleep, is your biggest devotee. Why is it so?'

Then the Lord says—'Narad ji, to make you understand I will have to do something. Will you obey an order of mine?'

Narad nods and says—'Definitely Your Lordship, I will always follow your command'.

Then the Lord says—'Take a bowl and fill it with oil to the brim. Put this oil-filled bowl on your palm and come back after taking seven rounds of the universe. And my order is that not a single drop of the oil should spill out of the bowl'.

Thinking that it is not such a tough job, Narad takes the bowl on his palm and starts doing rounds of the universe, fully attentive that no drop of oil spills out.

After completing the seven rounds Narad comes back to Lord Vishnu and says to him—'I am back and not a drop has spilled out'. At this the Lord asks him—'How many times did you utter my name?'

Narad says—'It was Your command that dominated my thoughts, in fact, my mind was focused entirely on the bowl lest a single drop of oil spills out. So I forgot to utter your name even once'.

At this the Lord says—'Now you know why the farmer is a greater and better devotee of mine than you. Whatever duties have been assigned to him, whether towards his family, towards the society, towards his fields or towards his cattle he fulfils with an implicit sense of responsibility. And even after doing that he doesn't forget to utter my name. So he is a greater worshiper than you as he is following orders of doing his duties and at the same time calling out my name, whereas you followed my order, yet forgot to utter my name'.

In reality this is the relation between religion and duty. Our duty is our biggest religion and the biggest worship. To fulfill your duty towards yourself, your family and towards all is the biggest worship. It is your work through which you can perform your duty. The greater the degree of your work, better the duty and higher the degree of your religiousness.

So no one should ever be under an illusion that religion is something different from the performance of duties.

RELIGION TO BE UNDERSTOOD IN THE CONTEXT OF DUTIES

Let me quote an example here. In our organization, Sahara India Pariwar, we greet each other by saying 'Sahara Pranam' (regard for Sahara). With this word, 'Sahara Pranam', the emotions of all our members are deeply attached. In official meetings all our workers assemble in a white shirt, a black pant and a black tie. We celebrate 'Bharat Parva' (Festival of 'Mother India') on 15th of August and 26th of January every year. All these have been adopted as rituals to kindle the constructive energies of the workers, along with infusing a sense of collectivism in them as in a 'Pariwar' or a family. These help maintain the flow of collective, creative energies which, in turn, generate productivity of a high degree. Collective productivity means collective interest, which means collective progress of all the workers with regard to money, respect and love and the sense of security being a continuous trend.

But if any worker of the organization coming to the office in a white shirt, a black pant and a black tie, keeps on saying 'Sahara Pranam' all day, and celebrates 'Bharat Parva' daily without doing any work, then you can very well imagine what will happen to the organization. Though our uniform, our greeting of 'Sahara Pranam' and our festival 'Bharat Parva' are all given prime importance with a lot of respect and love, the organization will still be compelled to remove such people as above, as they won't be giving any productivity.

In the same manner, to forge collective unity with a sense of emotionalism, we adopt and practise a number of rituals, we burn incense, make floral offerings, we offer prayer, ardaas, namaaz as per our individual customs and religious norms. One cannot deem it as improper to devote some time to these things, as it is quite appropriate for a human being to bow in total reverence before a religious deity. But out of ignorance these are observed as 'Dharma' or religion.

The religious rituals which have become prevalent in the name of religion, are proving to be very destructive to the society. To fight in the name of religion means to fight oneself meaning thereby, to create unnecessary emotional dissatisfaction for oneself. It is like someone throwing chilly powder in the eyes of others as well as his own and then all of them screaming together in pain. Should not people try to learn about religion, understand religious ethics, grasp them and adopt them? In all the religious scriptures, the ways of leading a good life have been laid down. We must try to understand them in the context of our duties. The stronger our intent in fulfilling our duties, the more beautiful will our life be.

Regarding the above, I recall an incident from my student days. Once, my father was scolding a lady who was the wife of the medical head of a factory.

My father was saying to the lady that hers was the greatest

act of sin towards her husband and the three sons [another son was in the army] as she never bothered to prepare breakfast, tiffin or lunch for them. She used to get up at 6 a.m. in the morning and continuously and passionately be involved 100% in worship, rituals. And her husband and all 3 sons were compelled to take care of themselves upto 2 p.m.

Well, that family was close to us all along.

You will be sad to know that that supremely religious mother first faced the death of her eldest son who was in the Army [owing to kidney failure], then the third son, the most promising one who died of cancer after a prolonged illness. I know of this as I was there at the time of the death and during the last breath, his head was on his most religious mother's lap. Then she lost her husband and subsequently the last blood in her life, when again in front of her eyes, the youngest son died in a road accident. She did not see her second son. The second son too has died of course, following his mother's death. Now you can well imagine what that woman achieved by neglecting her duties towards the family, in her obsession for rituals!

I do worship God for around 5 minutes everyday after my bath. I have not yet visited most of the popular temples, religious places.

In the last 30-40 years, I have visited temples and religious places twice at two different places without any work engagements. Of course, I have travelled extensively throughout my beloved country and my colleagues at times have taken me to a number of popular temples following my meetings etc.

But I am definitely one of the blessed children of God. It will be difficult for anyone to believe that during the late 60s when a four-wheeler used to be a big luxury, my father used to own three 04-wheelers. I used to keep those three 04-wheelers and one motor-cycle in my hostel. My father was very-very well placed.

We always lived in a high-class bungalow during my father's time. I remember the early 60s, when the entire household expense for a whole month used to be Rs. 100-150/-. At that time my father's salary used to about Rs. 4000/- plus and we had so many parties etc.

I always got the best and by God's blessings I still get the best of life.

There is a reason why I am writing so elaborately on this fact of my life, that I have yet to visit even once, many of the popular temples, religious places. Still, I am a supremely blessed child of God when compared to the millions who visit these temples, religious places, maybe 1-2-3 times every year.

You can ask my wife, other family members, my colleagues about their experience, of having observed me on a particular aspect—that I have never experienced mental tension ever in my life. I am always a happy person. I am truly God's blessed child.

Do you know why I have had this greatest blessing since my early days? It is due to my father, who was a great human-being.

I remember in the first week of every month, he used to spend an hour to send 15-20 money orders of different amounts to help in the running of families or for the education of so many youngsters.

He must have given (believe me) in lacs, personal loans to relatives and mainly junior colleagues during the 1960-70 decade.

He always used to tell me, "Son, don't have undue expectations of me, that I shall leave behind a house or a fat bank balance for you." Otherwise, he so rightly used to say that unless you struggle to develop your personality for a good, satisfying life, you shall never be able to taste the wonderful food God has given to us all. He again used to so rightly say that fathers who out of love and affection leave behind assets/ financial assets to their sons, actually out of ignorance turn them (the sons) into useless, lazy, non-productive people who just live out their lives without experiencing the greatest feeling of life that God has bestowed on us all.

Well, I would like to conclude this topic by repeatedly emphasizing upon the fact that for the continuous blessings of the Almighty, you have to follow His order—which is to perform all the best possible duties with kindness, dedication, enthusiastically towards mankind which He himself has created. Whatever be the sphere, you can help a needy person in matters of material or emotional support, giving the highest priority to performing genuine duties towards anybody and everybody, of course, by maintaining the balance of genuine duties towards oneself.

So wearing a uniform, greeting others with 'Sahara Pranam' is like a ritual (in Hindi we call it 'pooja padhdhati' that is, method of worship) but not religion as such.

Similarly going to a temple, offering flowers and lighting an incense stick, doing 'namaaz' in a masjid (mosque), doing ardas (Sikh way of praying) in gurudwaras, or prayers in Church are just rituals, methods of worship but not religion itself.

Religion is the performance of duty.

GENESIS OF RELIGION

For a while let us think of the period when there was only one man and one woman on the earth. Then they gave birth to their offspring; these offspring procreated further, and then the succession of procreation, thereby of population growth went on. There may have come a time when the place and the resources of livelihood fell short in proportion to population growth; so the people may have been compelled to migrate to different places.

At some point during the evolution, the intelligentsia of that time may have felt the need for formulating proper directives containing all the aspects of proper livelihood in order to organize properly, this collective human life and activity. In order to make a better community, the wise people may have formulated rules and regulations keeping in mind the basic nature of human beings. Thus they may have set directives and persuaded the people to follow these directives by causing a fear of the powers of Nature in them. They might have caused fear in them so as to make people adopt those directives religiously and respectfully for the betterment of the community. Human society may have evolved on these lines.

EMERGENCE OF A RELIGIOUS ORDER

Having moulded life according to the formulated rules, regulations and directives (in every religion only one way has been defined to lead a successful life, however the expressions of it have been different) humans must have benefited from them and they might have continued adopting them.

While the process of migration across geographical boundaries was going on, people might have taken the sets of rules, regulations, ethics and rituals to their respective new places. In those times there were not such advanced communication and transportation systems as are today. So the rules, regulations and ethics did not spread across the world uniformly. Consequently different religions and sects emerged at different places, and different systems and social orders were generated.

At the same time we will have to realize the fact that the different sets of rules, regulations, morals and ethics that evolved in different communities took the shape of organized religions. In this way different religions came into existence. People got emotionally attached to their respective religions and took their supreme beings as a form of Ishwar, God, Allah, etc. In the process people identified themselves with their different religions and their different identities became of paramount importance for them.

So it is seen these days that people are very much attached to their respective religions, and the fact that they all are the offspring of the same progenitor, has gone into the background.

THE SOLUTION IS TO ESTABLISH A 'NATIONAL RELIGION'

Here the question arises that in a multi-ethnic country like India, how to inculcate a religious faith in people of all religions so that everybody fulfils their responsibilities towards the society and the nation, at large. This can be achieved through the concept of a **'National Religion'**.

If this concept in essence is understood by all religious followers, then not only would we see the establishment of a proper religious system, but also get rid of communal tensions and disturbances to a large extent.

Let me make it clear that for this, we need not undermine any other religious belief. The Constitution should be suitably amended so that a national religion may be created, inclusive of all religions.

By compiling all the good aspects of various religions, by combining duty with religion and by disseminating the notion of a national religion, not only would a solution be found to religious disputes but our nation could be developed as a strong and progressive one.

Let me take this up in some detail.

HOW DOES ONE FORMULATE A NATIONAL RELIGION?

In India the word 'Hindu' has been wrongly taken as a synonym for religion. The word Hindu came into existence because of the river 'Sindhu'. In Persian language 'H' was the sound for 'S', so Sindhu turned into Hindu. 'Hindu' is not a religion whereas 'Vaishnav', 'Sanatan' are religions.

The term 'Hindu' has no relation to religion; however many beautiful ways of living a community life have been devised in Hinduism, so it follows a set direction, particularly where there is an amalgamation of religions. Since the very beginning the Hindu system has been able to provide an emotional base. Sikhs, Buddhists and Jains, etc., have been associated with the Hindu system of living.

So even for the Muslim brethren, as there is a preponderance of the Hindu system in India, there may be a way of getting long-lasting peace, happiness and satisfaction in abundance within the system. As Hinduism is a way of life, the Muslim brethren need not disassociate themselves from their own religious beliefs. This is just an association with a particular way of life. Though it is not necessary to accept Hinduism, one thing is imperative, and that is the formation of some kind of a single religion for sound nation-building. So, for India, only a 'national religion' may provide an alternative.

If you think carefully you will not disagree with me. We need not demean any religion. Yet by taking all the religions together and making a few changes in each, a national religion could be formulated. Under the rule of the land, there have to be uniform rules and regulations applicable to every citizen of the nation. For any nation, there should not be different codes of conduct based on different religions. So to implement this concept, it is a must that a national religion is formulated by embracing the nation as a family. However impossible it may appear, it must be done.

For all the people of this nation, as far as possible, uniformity should be brought about in the ways of living and in the customs and conventions. In the name of religion the primary duty of everyone must be to work towards national interest. In the period of Akbar, 'Deen-E-Ilahi' also mentions the national religion propounding interfaith harmony. Because of 'Deen'-E'-Ilahi', Akbar's period of rule is known to be the most prudent and progressive, where there was peace, happiness and prosperity in abundance.

NATIONAL INTEREST IS PARAMOUNT

If today the population of the country has crossed the dangerous one billion mark, the followers of all the religions, considering national interest as the supreme religion, will have to come forward to reduce the load of population by giving birth to as less children as possible.

In addition, to keep the nation beautiful it will be vital that 'Pooja', 'Ardas', "Ibadat' are performed only within the homes. Outside their homes, all citizens must follow the national religion and remain Indians alone. Publicly, our festivals would be the 15th of August and the 26th of January, i.e., the Independence Day and the Republic Day.

The inspirational sources of national religion would be luminaries like Gandhiji, Subhash Chandra Bose, Maulana Abul Kalam Azad, Chandrashekhar Azad, Bhagat Singh etc. These great personalities and their deeds and thoughts could offer a wide range of human virtues and values for generating faith in establishing a national religion, which can provide a strong base for strengthening our emotional unity. If it so happens, with the passage of time we will see a beautiful form of our national unity emerging.

THE NEED FOR A CONSTRUCTIVE MOVEMENT

To give a concrete shape to this concept, whether one is Hindu or Muslim, a Sikh or a Christian, all will have to come forward to launch a constructive movement. People should not lose their lives or their peace, happiness and satisfaction by being swept away by the so-called intellectuals or flag bearers of the religions.

The political leaders are unfortunately entangled in vote-bank politics and the intellectuals and religious leaders are motivated by their narrow self interests. So their speeches may momentarily appear joyful, attractive and laden with sympathy, but their long term impact is always disastrous for a society like the Indian. Therefore, owing to not thinking about or accepting the basic realities in our country, if we fail to unite then even 'Ishwar' and 'Allah' will not be able to help us, leave alone bless us.

A lot of religious scriptures are available in our country. Religious scriptures mean the written codes of duties i.e. the sermons instructing how, why and when you can fulfill your duties beautifully and productively in order to make your life beautiful forever. But as we all know, for the common man all such religious scriptures have become objects of bowing his head to, in reverence.

If today a new scripture is compiled for the peace, happiness and satisfaction of the masses, it will prove very effective. According to the modern context, all the relevant teachings from the Geeta, the Vedas, the Quran, the Bible, and the Guru Granth Sahib should be taken and compiled into one scripture, but should be enhanced from an entirely new perspective, which should then be introduced in the modern Indian education system from the primary level.

IN CONCLUSION

India since centuries has been known for its religious diversity and to practise one's own beliefs is enshrined in our Constitution as a fundamental right. As a secular republic, therefore, the rights of the citizens need to be upheld to freely worship or propagate any religion, faith or creed as per individual choice.

However, I am of the firm opinion that the interests of the nation are paramount and should always be placed above religion and all religious beliefs. I strongly believe that to preserve and propagate the rich emotional unity of our large Indian family and reinforce the spirit of 'unity within diversity', a 'National Religion' is truly essential as it would bring about a social integration of all our religious beliefs, customs and rituals, thus providing a strong impetus to healthy and collective emotional co-existence. This would also go a long way in serving the cause of building a stronger, a united and a much more prosperous India.

A HUMBLE APPEAL

I shall be thankful, grateful if you send in your valuable feedback in case of any disagreement on any aspect of the book, on any questions that may arise in your mind, any suggestions you may have, after having gone through its contents.

You can submit your valuable feedback by visiting www.saharasri.in (my personal website) or www.saharasribooks.in

Alternately, you can also submit the above by email on: feedback-thinkwithme@saharasribooks.in